Dedication

This book is dedicated to you dear reader, for making this journey worthwhile. Haven, who inspires me to keep writing, my family and all those who decided to give my book a chance.

Thank you and love always.

Haven was a curious and adventurous 5-year-old girl. One sunny morning, Haven woke up with a big smile. "Today is the day!" Haven said, jumping out of bed. Today, Haven was going to visit a farm for the first time.

Haven had learned about farms in school. Her teacher taught her about farm animals and farm tools and she became curious about farms since then. At home, mom and dad promised to take Haven to see a nearby farm on Saturday. She has been very excited since then.

"Hurry up, Haven!" called Mom from downstairs. Haven quickly got dressed and ran down. The family was all ready to go. Dad was packing a picnic basket, and little brother Leo was playing with his toy tractor.

Let's go!" said Dad, smiling. They all hopped into the car. Haven couldn't sit still. "What will the farm be like?" Haven wondered aloud. The car ride seemed to take forever, but finally, they arrived at Farmer Joe's farm.

The farm was vast, stretching as far as the eye could see. Tall green grass swayed gently in the breeze. In the distance, Haven could see a big red barn with white trim, its paint slightly faded from the sun. Next to it was a small farmhouse painted bright yellow with white shutters and a wrap-around porch. A white picket fence surrounded the farm, the wood smooth and freshly painted. Beyond the fence, there were fields of golden corn and rows of leafy vegetables. The smell of fresh hay mixed with the earthy scent of the soil filled the air.

Haven took a deep breath, enjoying the rich, warm smell. The sounds of the farm were like music. From afar, Haven could hear the mooing of cows, the clucking of chickens, and the oinking of pigs. Birds chirped merrily in the trees, and somewhere a rooster crowed loudly, announcing their arrival.

Farmer Joe greeted them with a big smile. He wore a straw hat that shaded his weathered face, and he had a friendly dog named Buddy by his side. Buddy was a big, fluffy dog with a wagging tail and soft brown eyes.

"Welcome to the farm, Haven!" said Farmer Joe. His voice was warm and cheerful. Buddy barked happily and wagged his tail even more.
"Hi, Farmer Joe! Hi, Buddy!" said Haven, bending down to pet the dog. Buddy's fur was soft and warm under Haven's hand, and he gave Haven's face a big, wet lick. Haven giggled.

Haven's heart was pounding with excitement. The farm was even bigger than imagined. Chickens roamed freely, pecking at the ground, and cows grazed lazily in the fields. Pigs rolled in the mud, snorting contentedly, and sheep bleated as they nibbled on the grass.
"This place is amazing!" said Haven, her eyes sparkling with wonder.
"Let me show you around," said Farmer Joe. "There's lots to see and do here."

Haven's family followed Farmer Joe past the farmhouse, noticing the wooden swing hanging from an old oak tree and the bright red tractor parked near the barn. Haven couldn't wait to see everything and learn all about the farm.

First, they went to the chicken coop. The chicken coop was a little wooden house with a fence around it. Inside, chickens of different colors were busy pecking at the ground. "Cluck, cluck!" they said. Some chickens were white, some were brown, and some were black and white.

"These are the chickens," said Farmer Joe. "They give us eggs."

Haven watched as a white chicken laid a smooth, brown egg. "Wow!" said Haven, eyes wide with wonder. "Can I hold it?"

Farmer Joe handed Haven the warm egg. It felt smooth and a little bit heavy in Haven's hand. "It's so warm," said Haven, smiling.

Next, they saw the cows. The cows were big and gentle, with soft brown and black fur. "Moo!" said a big brown cow.
"This is Bessie," said Farmer Joe. "She gives us milk. I will show you how."
Farmer Joe took a shiny metal bucket and placed it under the cow. He began to milk the cow. Haven watched as Farmer Joe milked Bessie. The milk squirted into the shiny metal bucket with a funny sound. "Squirt, squirt!"

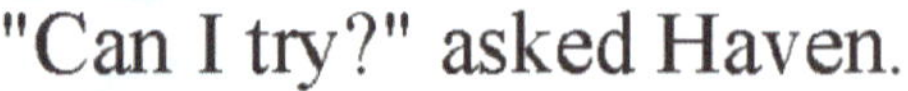

"Can I try?" asked Haven.
Farmer Joe showed Haven how to milk the cow. Haven giggled as the milk squirted into the bucket. It was warm and white. "This is fun!" said Haven.

Then, they went to see the pigs. The pigs were medium-sized and had pink, smooth skin. They were much smaller than the cow. They were rolling in the mud, snorting happily. "Oink, oink!" they said.
"These are the pigs," said Farmer Joe. "They love to play in the mud."

One little piglet, named Pip, came up to Haven. Pip was tiny and had the cutest little snout. "Hello, Pip!" said Haven, patting the piglet's head. Pip snorted happily and wiggled its tail.
After that, they saw the sheep. The sheep were fluffy and white, grazing in the green field. "Baa, baa!" they said.

"These are the sheep," said Farmer Joe. "They give us wool."
Haven touched the soft wool on a sheep named Woolly. Woolly's wool felt
like a soft, cozy blanket. "It's so fluffy!" said Haven, smiling.

Finally, they visited the barn and saw the horses. The horses were tall and strong, with shiny coats. "Neigh!" said a big brown horse.
"This is Star," said Farmer Joe. "I ride on it around the farm."
Haven looked at Star's shiny coat and strong legs. Star's coat was a beautiful brown, and his mane was black and shiny. "He's beautiful!" said Haven, admiring the big horse.
Each animal was special in its own way, and Haven loved meeting them all.

Farmer Joe showed Haven some farm tools. The first tool was a pitchfork. It had a long wooden handle and four sharp metal prongs. "This is a pitchfork," said Farmer Joe. "We use it to move hay."

Farmer Joe demonstrated by sticking the pitchfork into a pile of hay and lifting it up. The hay made a rustling sound as it moved. "See how it works?" he asked.

Haven tried to lift the pitchfork. It was big and a little heavy. "It's heavy!" said Haven, laughing. The handle felt rough and strong in Haven's hands. "But it's fun!"

Next, Farmer Joe showed Haven a shovel. The shovel had a metal blade and a wooden handle. "This is a shovel," said Farmer Joe. "We use it to dig."
Farmer Joe showed Haven how to dig a hole in the ground. The shovel went into the dirt with a crunching sound. "We use the shovel to plant seeds and dig up potatoes," he explained.
Haven used a smaller shovel to dig in the dirt. The small shovel was just the right size and not too heavy. "Digging is fun!" said Haven, scooping up the soil. The dirt felt cool and soft.

Finally, Farmer Joe showed Haven the tractor. The tractor was big and green, with large black tires. It had a seat, a steering wheel, and pedals. "This is a tractor," said Farmer Joe. "It helps us plow the fields and carry heavy things."

Farmer Joe climbed into the tractor and started the engine. The tractor made a loud, rumbling sound. "Vroom, vroom!" said Haven, covering their ears. "Would you like to sit in the seat?" asked Farmer Joe.

Haven climbed into the tractor seat. It was high up and felt powerful. Haven put hands on the steering wheel. "Vroom, vroom!" said Haven, pretending to drive. Farmer Joe laughed. "You make a good farmer, Haven!" he said. Each tool was special and important for different jobs on the farm. Haven learned how hard and fun it was to work on a farm.

Suddenly, Haven noticed something. "Where's Pip?" asked Haven. The little piglet was not in the pen.
Farmer Joe looked worried. "Pip often wanders off," he said. "We need to find him before he gets into trouble."
"I'll help!" said Haven. "Let's find Pip." Haven, Buddy, and Farmer Joe started searching the farm.

They looked in the barn. "Pip, where are you?" called Haven. But there was no sign of Pip. They searched the fields. "Pip!" shouted Farmer Joe. But still, no Pip.

They looked near the chicken coop and the cow pen. "Do you see any clues, Buddy?" asked Haven. Buddy sniffed around and barked.

"Look, muddy footprints!" said Haven. They followed the footprints to the vegetable garden.

Haven heard a faint squealing sound. "Pip!" called Haven. They found Pip stuck in a muddy ditch. Pip was squealing and wiggling, unable to get out.
"Oh no, Pip!" said Haven. "We need to help him."

Farmer Joe tried to reach Pip, but the ditch was too deep. "Haven, can you help me?" asked Farmer Joe.
Haven nodded bravely. "I'll try!" Haven crawled into the ditch carefully. The mud was sticky.
"Come here, Pip," said Haven gently. Pip wiggled closer. Haven grabbed Pip and lifted him up. Farmer Joe pulled them both out of the ditch.

Pip was safe! "You did it, Haven!" said Farmer Joe. Haven was covered in mud, but smiling.
Pip snorted happily and licked Haven's face. "You're welcome, Pip," said Haven, laughing.

They took Pip back to the pen. The other pigs were happy to see Pip. "Oink, oink!" they said.

Farmer Joe was very grateful. "Thank you, Haven," he said. "You are a hero!" They decided to have a picnic to celebrate.
Mom and Dad set up a blanket under a big tree. They brought out sandwiches, apples, and cookies. Farmer Joe brought fresh milk and eggs from the farm. "This is delicious!" said Haven, biting into a crisp apple. The fresh milk was creamy and sweet. Buddy sat next to Haven, hoping for a treat.

As the sun began to set, it was time to say goodbye. Haven petted the chickens, cows, pigs, sheep, and horses one last time. "Goodbye, everyone!" said Haven. "I'll miss you!"

Farmer Joe gave Haven a special farm hat. "This is for you, Haven," he said. "Come back and visit us soon."

"I will!" said Haven, putting on the hat. Haven felt very happy and proud.

On the way home, Haven couldn't stop talking about the farm. "I met so many animals and learned so much!" said Haven. "And I rescued Pip!"
Mom and Dad smiled. "We are so proud of you, Haven," said Mom. "You were very brave."

Haven yawned, feeling tired but happy. "I can't wait to tell my friends," said Haven, closing her eyes.
Haven dreamed of the farm, the animals, and the adventures. It was the best day ever, and Haven knew they would visit the farm again soon.

www.ingramcontent.com/pod-product-compliance
Lightning Source LLC
Chambersburg PA
CBHW040204240726
48664CB00002B/833